# CHAPTER 1: MASTERING THE ART OF EMBROIDERY

Embroidery: The Artistry Woven in Threads

In the realm of fabric transformation, embroidery reigns as a timeless craft that bestows intricate beauty upon materials through the delicate dance of threads and needles. This meticulous artistry involves adorning fabrics and other mediums with threads or yarns, often enhanced with pearls, beads, sequins, and quills, to create awe-inspiring designs. Notable symbols of this artistry include the iconic Ralph Lauren logo and the maritime elegance of the Nautica emblem.

Pros and Cons: The Dichotomy of Embroidery

Pros:

- Accessibility: Low minimum requirements open doors for businesses of all scales to indulge in this art form.
- Colorful Expression: The number of colors within your design does not dictate an increase in cost.

Cons:

- Magnitude Matters: Elaborate designs can amplify costs.
- Weighty Elegance: Larger designs on lighter garments can compromise comfort.
- Fine Detail Dilemma: The artistry's finesse can be lost in translation.

The Artisan's Dilemma: DIY or Outsource Embroidery?

Similar to screen printing, mastering embroidery necessitates appropriate equipment and skill. The aspiration of a DIY venture requires a significant investment in equipment and supplies, with embroidery machines starting at $10,000 or more. For efficiency and brand focus, outsourcing embroidery is often recommended. This allows creators to channel their efforts into brand marketing while skilled artisans embellish the fabric canvas.

Crafting Embroidered Art: A Fusion of Creativity and Technique

When envisioning designs for embroidery, creators must navigate certain considerations. The medium's inherent limitations make replicating complex digital prints, with intricate details and gradients, a challenge. The primary essence lies in the marriage of thread and fabric, necessitating thoughtful artistry.

Vector artwork becomes the guiding principle, ensuring a crisp digitized embroidery file. Simple graphic elements—typography logos, vector line art, and minimalist cartoon depictions—thrive in this realm.

## Demystifying Digitization: The Language of Stitches

Embroidery's journey from art to reality hinges on digitization, which transmutes designs into a language machines understand. Digitizers—essentially artists—are entrusted with this transformation, ensuring precision in stitch placement. The process equates to redrawing logos or designs into stitch formations using specialized software. Clean digital files ensure exact placement, enhancing the final embroidered outcome. Adobe Illustrator or high-resolution Photoshop files are recommended, although other formats can be adapted.

## Backing Paper: The Unseen Foundation

Behind the scenes of embroidery lies a crucial yet hidden component: stabilizer or backing paper. This foundation provides the necessary substrate for the threads to cling to, elevating the design. Tear-away, cutaway, and water-soluble stabilizers present varied options, catering to fabric type, stitch density, and design stability.

The interaction between backing and thread is pivotal, impacting the final aesthetic quality.

## From Concept to Clothing: Decoding Pricing Variables

Embroidery pricing converges around three dominant variables:

> Stitch Count and Size: Designs are often priced by stitch count, leading to larger designs incurring higher costs.
> Location: Unique design placements might attract additional charges due to complexity.
> Thread Palette: Embroiderers stock common threads, necessitating custom orders for specific colors.

## Leveraging Pricing Strategies: A Crafty Approach

Strategic ordering can optimize pricing, especially when navigating quantity-based discounts. Analyzing price charts unveils the breakpoints that yield maximum savings. Efficiently deploying capital to yield the best value becomes the focus, avoiding the pitfalls of excess inventory. Efficient pricing offers balance while bolstering cash flow.

## Beyond Embroidery: The Print-On-Demand Frontier

For budding entrepreneurs, embracing a print-on-demand strategy offers an avenue for launching a brand with minimal financial commitment. The approach entails selling custom-designed products via online stores, with third-party vendors handling manufacturing and shipping. This model eliminates inventory costs and mitigates risks, providing a viable entry point for creativity-driven ventures.

## Packaging: The Final Flourish

Packaging isn't mere logistics; it's an extension of your brand experience. Poly bags shield garments during storage, preserving their integrity until they're ready for the world. Next, the packaging journey branches into two routes:

>Poly Mailers: Cost-effective and versatile, these lightweight mailers are perfect for startup brands. Customization options range from stickers to themed designs.
>Box Mailers: Elevate the unboxing experience with these more premium options. They exude professionalism

and can be customized to mirror your brand aesthetic.

Tailoring the Journey: A Personalized Touch

Small details, like folded garments and hang tags, convey attention to detail. Custom hang tags bolster brand recognition, while size stickers enhance organization. Stickers, from branded logos to playful add-ons, inject delight into the unboxing ritual.

Innovative Engagement: Going the Extra Mile

To transcend conventional packaging, consider unconventional inclusions:

- Artful candy assortments
- Unique air fresheners
- Mini collectibles
- Customized stickers
- And beyond...

From Craft to Commerce: Navigating Sales and Marketing

To thrive in the competitive landscape, mastering sales and marketing is essential:

- Craft a compelling brand story
- Leverage social media to foster a community
- Collaborate with influencers to amplify reach
- Employ email marketing to nurture relationships
- Optimize your online store for seamless shopping

Embroidery, beyond being an art, transforms into a vehicle of expression. It's a tapestry woven from creativity, technique, and a deep connection to the fabric of your brand. With each intricate stitch, your story evolves, bridging the realms of fashion and artistry.

# CHAPTER 2:
# ELEVATING FASHION
# THROUGH SCREEN
# PRINTING MASTERY

*Unveiling the Artistry and Innovation of Modern Apparel Decoration*

In the ever-evolving landscape of fashion, a craft thrives that holds the power to transform garments into wearable masterpieces—screen printing. This centuries-old technique has taken on new life, becoming the linchpin of contemporary self-expression. From the iconic 'Just Do It' Nike tees to intricate hoodie designs, screen printing is the secret sauce that gives fashion its unique flavor.

Decoding the Enigma: The Intricacies of Screen Printing

Peer behind the curtain of screen printing, and you'll discover a world of meticulous artistry and technique. Imagine each hue of your design requiring a separate mesh stencil. These stencils are then delicately aligned, like a conductor orchestrating the elements of a symphony, ensuring each color finds its place. The inks are then gently coaxed onto the fabric, and the masterpiece is subjected to a precise curing process, forever etching the design into the textile.

Colors as a Language of Expression

The color palette of screen printing is like an artist's palette, brimming with possibilities. Traditional plastisol ink offers durability and sharpness, while water-based ink introduces a tactile softness. For those seeking to push boundaries, discharge ink fuses pigment with fabric, making it an ideal choice for cotton garments.

Choreographing Design and Placement

Design placement is a choreography of innovation. Each strategic location on the garment adds layers of intrigue and nuance, but it's also a dance with costs. The interplay between design impact and budget constraints becomes a delicate balance. Specialty placements hold an allure, but they may come at an added cost due to their intricacy.

From Vision to Reality: Crafting Wearable Art

This convergence of fabric, ink, and design is where dreams are made tangible.

Harnessing the Power of Pantone

Enter the Pantone Matching System, the lexicon of color precision. Pantone codes serve as the bridge between imagination and reality. Each code signifies a shade, creating a universal language for hues that transcends mere aesthetics.

Navigating the Economics of Expression

Deciphering pricing transforms creators into savvy economists. The intricacy of the design, the number of colors, and placement —all these elements have financial implications. Quantity becomes a formidable ally, driving costs downward as volumes surge. Amid the numerical labyrinth, the true worth of the endeavor resides in the enchantment of the design, for each print captures a fragment of the creator's vision.

A Tale of Two Printers: Partners in Creation

In the realm of screen printing, two archetypes emerge—the retail printer and the contract/wholesale printer. The former thrives on high-margin, low-volume projects, while the latter banks on economies of scale to cater to higher-volume needs.

Recognizing these distinctions empowers creators to select the partner aligned with their vision and goals.

Empowerment through Creation: A DIY Odyssey

For those who dare to embark on the DIY journey, a universe of potential opens up. Armed with a heat press and plastisol screen printed transfers, creators can sculpt their designs into reality without breaking the bank. This empowering strategy bridges the gap between inspiration and affordability, making self-expression attainable for all.

A Finale of Creativity: Designs that Speak Volumes

Screen printing isn't merely a technique—it's an instrument of narrative. Every stroke of the squeegee, every color merge, every press through the dryer breathes life into the design. Screen printing immortalizes creativity on fabric, transforming garments into sagas yearning to be worn and shared.

# CHAPTER 3: EXPLORING THE WORLD OF DESIGN

*Diving into the Journey of Design Making and Collaboration*

In a realm full of possibilities, the field of design has changed a lot, becoming a crucial part of brand identity and self-expression. Whether it's creating a logo or coming up with cool merchandise designs, the process of telling stories through visuals has become an exciting blend of creativity and new ideas.

Navigating Through the Process: Creating Something Special with Design

Getting into design is like going on an adventure, where creativity and new thinking come together. Whether you're working on a logo, thinking about colors, or figuring out design theory, the journey to create a unique identity is like exploring new territory.

Talking the Design Talk: Making Your Vision a Reality

When it comes to making a logo, it's like directing a group of ideas and images. This involves not just talking to designers but also figuring out who's really good at this and learning some tips to make your design journey smoother.

It's about making the right choice without blowing your budget. Finding that balance between hiring a good designer and not spending too much money is important. Online platforms like Fiverr can be really useful here, letting you find talented designers who can start working for you with just a small investment.

Understanding Designers: Telling the Stars from the Rest

Finding a great designer is a bit like a treasure hunt, where you're looking for certain clues and qualities. There are some clear signs that someone is great at what they do. On the other hand, there are also signs that someone might not be the best fit. It's like sorting the gems from the rocks.

*The Awesome Designers*: These are the ones who have their own unique style that's consistent in all their work. They often start with hand-drawn art and then turn it into digital designs. They don't rely on stock images and they really understand colors and how things should look. They're more interested in creating great art than just getting paid, and they usually have lots of repeat customers.

*The Not-So-Great Designers*: These designers might use stock images and slap them together to create something. They might not be very familiar with professional design software like Adobe Photoshop or Illustrator. They lack a good understanding of design basics and often don't have much of a portfolio to show. They tend to focus more on making money and might not value their work as much.

Champion Designers: A Gallery of Brilliant Minds

As the world of design expands, there are some exceptional designers who shine bright. They're the ones who craft brand logos with finesse and turn wearable items into pieces of art.

*Logo Heroes*: These are the folks who create logos that really capture a brand's essence. *Merchandise Mavericks*: They're the wizards behind cool designs on clothes and accessories.

Creating Wearable Tales: Making Stories Come Alive

Beyond logos, there's a whole world of designing merchandise, like t-shirts and hats. It's about taking your imagination and making it work with different ways of printing. Embroidery and screen printing are two different methods, each with its own style.

Embroidery involves stitching and thread, and works best with simpler designs. Screen printing is all about vibrant designs and works better for more intricate artwork.

The Plan of Action: Guiding Your Designer

When you're working with a designer, good communication is key. Give them a clear plan by creating a PDF with your ideas. This will help them understand what you're looking for and bring your vision to life. It's like giving them a roadmap to follow.

Exploring New Avenues: Finding More Design Talent

While Fiverr is a great starting point, there are other ways to find talented designers. Platforms like Behance are like hubs for creative work. Social media, like Instagram and Twitter, is also full of designers waiting to be discovered. You can even use sites like Craigslist to find designers.

Your Own Design Adventure: Learning the Ropes

Remember, you have the power to shape your brand's look. Even if you're not a designer, you can learn some basics and try things out. It's like a journey of discovery that can add a unique touch to your brand.

## In Conclusion: The World of Visual Stories

Design isn't just about making things look nice; it's about telling stories through visuals. From logos to merchandise, every design choice adds a layer of meaning to your brand. As design keeps evolving, embracing new ideas and possibilities, it continues to be a powerful way to communicate and connect with others.

# CHAPTER 4: FORGING YOUR BRAND'S PATH

*Blueprinting Your Brand: The Odyssey Ahead*

In the dynamic landscape of fashion and branding, crafting your distinct brand unfolds like an exhilarating adventure. This chapter unveils the stages of igniting your brand idea, sculpting its character, and translating your vision into tangible designs.

Breathing Life into Ideas: Carving a Passage

Before delving into the intricacies of garment printing and designer collaborations, it's imperative to paint a vivid picture of your brand's essence. This initial phase lays the foundation for your brand's identity, propelling it towards its destined direction.

*Defining Your Brand Essence*: While birthing a single design is remarkable, crafting a brand necessitates a symphony of designs that stand the test of time. Consider the essence of your brand— its core message, its audience, and the unique vibes it radiates.

Embarking on Persona Crafting: Carving Identity

A brand persona serves as a mirror reflecting your brand's values, personality, and identity. Think of it as an individual who intimately embodies your brand. Crafting a compelling persona fosters a deeper bond with your audience, kindling resonance and loyalty.

*Harnessing Brand Persona Power*: Beyond aesthetics, an authentic brand persona fosters trust and engagement. Sculpting a persona breathes life into your communication strategy. For e-commerce, a well-forged persona can be the wind beneath your sales' wings.

Narrating the Brand Tale: The Heartbeat of Your Identity

Every brand conceals a story within its fibers. Unearthing your brand's origin story, the driving force behind it, and its style or vibe creates an intimate connection with your audience.

*Infusing Depth into Your Brand*: By narrating the inception of your brand, its essence, and the driving passion, you add layers to your products. Whether sparked by a personal journey or a singular inspiration, your brand's narrative breathes life into its identity.

Architecting Purpose: Crafting Vision and Mission Statements

Crafting concise yet impactful vision and mission statements encapsulates your brand's ambitions and purpose. A vision statement casts a light on your brand's aspirations, while a mission statement fleshes out your offering and distinctiveness.

*Vision Statements*: These succinct declarations illuminate your brand's path over years, providing a compass for your journey. Examples across sectors illustrate the art of encapsulating profound visions.

*Mission Statements*: Delve into specifics with a mission statement that outlines your brand's unique offerings and target market. It's your roadmap to achieving the grand vision.

Plotting the Trajectory: Goals and Budgeting

Just as every adventure demands a map, your brand's journey requires well-defined goals. Employ the S.M.A.R.T. (Specific, Measurable, Attainable, Relevant, Timely) formula to set milestones. Simultaneously, draft a budget covering launch expenses and long-term sustainability.

By adhering to this formula, your goals take tangible shape, ensuring alignment with your brand's essence.

*Budgeting for Triumph*: Allocating resources smartly, from packaging to product creation, safeguards quality and sustenance. Balancing costs ensures a strong foundation for your brand.

Sketched Blueprints: Forging a Comprehensive Business Strategy

With your brand's core etched in your mind, it's time to translate concepts into a comprehensive business plan. This document crystallizes your brand's essence, strategy, and financial roadmaps, fostering clarity and consistency.

*Organizing the Vision*: Converting your brand's diverse facets into writing lends structure and direction. A well-constructed business plan offers a holistic view on a single canvas.

Fabric's Transformation: The Odyssey of Garment Selection

Armed with your brand's identity, it's time to breathe life into your vision through garments. Discern the choices between pre-made blanks and cut & sew garments, pathways that pave the way for your brand's unique expression.

*Pre-Made Blanks*: Established clothing entities offer raw canvases for your designs. These are the building blocks for your creative endeavor, offering flexibility and low minimum orders.

*Cut & Sew Adventure*: Venturing into the world of creating garments from scratch opens doors to unparalleled creativity. Be prepared for a higher investment and deeper resource involvement.

Quality Chronicles: Navigating Garment Excellence

The quality of your garments mirrors your brand's essence. Stick to first-quality merchandise for consistency and dependable supplier relationships. While closeouts and irregulars hold allure, they come with their considerations.

*First Quality Triumph*: Retail-ready garments meet stringent quality benchmarks, ensuring consistency and trust in your brand. Count on reliable stock for your brand's evolution.

*Closeouts and Irregulars Temptation*: While enticing for bargains, these categories warrant caution. Closeouts offer discounted excess inventory, but reordering is unlikely. Irregulars demand scrutiny as their defects may impact your brand's reputation.

Identity Seal with Neck Labels: Elevating Professionalism

Elevate your brand's finesse by customizing neck labels. Be it weaving, printing, or heat transfers, these labels imprint your brand's identity on each piece, adding a touch of professionalism.

*Neck Labels Impact*: Often overlooked, neck labels wield immense power. Personalized labels add an air of sophistication, though costs and procedures must be weighed wisely.

Navigating Supplier Avenues: Blank Garment Sources

Navigating the realm of blank garment suppliers may seem overwhelming. Opt for trusted industry stalwarts such as S&S Activewear, Alphabroder, Carolina Made, and more. Remember, each supplier has distinct strengths and cautions.

Epilogue: Unveiling Your Brand's Odyssey

From idea inception to garment realization, your brand's journey is a testament to creativity, resilience, and foresight. Every stitch, every decision is a brushstroke in a canvas narrating your brand's tale, resonating with those attuned to your unique essence. Remember, the journey itself enriches the destination.

# CHAPTER 5: ORCHESTRATING UNFORGETTABLE BRAND EXPERIENCES

*Elevating Your Brand's Narrative Symphony*

Enter the realm where brand storytelling and community harmonize, crafting a symphony of engagement and loyalty. In this chapter, discover how the narrative threads that bind your brand's story with the aspirations of your community can birth profound connections and lasting allegiances.

Melodies of Resonance: Crafting Brand Stories that Echo

Within every brand lies a narrative waiting to reverberate across hearts. Unveil the nuances of composing a captivating brand story—a tale that resonates with your audience, stitching shared values, experiences, and aspirations.

*The Anatomy of Resonance*: Drench your brand's story in authenticity, painting a canvas of real experiences, challenges, and triumphs. Conveying vulnerability and authenticity lends authenticity, forging an indelible bond with your audience.

Epic Narratives: From Antiquity to Modernity

Exploring storytelling's archaic roots unveils the perennial magic it wields. Learn from both the ancients and the contemporaries as you mold your brand's narrative, fusing classic storytelling elements with contemporary relevance.

*The Hero's Journey*: Journey through mythic archetypes and the hero's quest, imbuing your brand's narrative with timeless grandeur. From the ordinary world to the call to adventure, every step forms a tapestry that captivates and compels.

Engagement Crescendos: Forging Community Bonds

Amplify your brand's resonance by nurturing a dedicated community. Transitioning passive consumers into fervent brand advocates requires a strategic blend of engagement platforms, content, and shared values.

*Energizing Your Tribe*: Online forums, social media groups, and interactive events cultivate a sense of belonging. Communities thrive when fueled by shared passion and a platform for genuine dialogue.

Captivating Collaborations: The Art of Co-Creation

Enrich your brand's tapestry through strategic collaborations that encompass creativity, cross-promotion, and community expansion. Crafting symbiotic partnerships extends your brand's reach while creating novel experiences for your audience.

*Collaborative Alchemy*: Melding artistic prowess with

entrepreneurial finesse, collaborations birth limited-edition collections, brand partnerships, and special events. The result? An enriched narrative that captivates and surprises.

Creating Interactive Soirées: Events that Transcend

Engage your community in immersive experiences that transcend traditional transactions. Whether through pop-up shops, interactive workshops, or live events, these soirées fuse tactile engagement with brand loyalty.

*Pop-Up Poetry*: Transient yet impactful, pop-up shops breathe life into the digital realm, fostering personal connections and tactile engagement. These physical rendezvous spaces not only showcase your products but infuse them with stories and personalities.

Sustainment Harmonies: Nurturing Long-Term Engagement

Maintaining your community's ardor requires sustained engagement strategies. These include exclusive memberships, loyalty programs, and educational content that cater to your audience's ongoing growth.

*The Encore Effect*: Harnessing the essence of anticipation, loyalty programs offer exclusive rewards, sneak peeks, and early access to your offerings. The sense of belonging deepens, and your audience transforms into fervent patrons.

Strategies of Audible Resonance: Crafting Sonic Branding

Unveiling the art of sonic branding reveals the uncharted world of audio recognition. Melodies, jingles, and even voice commands serve as auditory extensions of your brand, triggering instant associations in the minds of your audience.

*In the Echoes of Sound*: Sonic branding creates a sensory identity that bridges the gap between auditory perception and brand recognition. A harmonious jingle or a distinctive audio logo enhances your brand's recall value and adds a layer of immersion.

The Symphony of User-Generated Content: Amplifying Community Voices

Harnessing the power of user-generated content, this chapter navigates the avenues through which your community members can actively contribute to your brand's narrative. Transform your consumers into collaborators.

*Vocalizing the Audience*: User-generated content empowers your community to become co-creators. Social media challenges, hashtags, and contests turn your audience into active storytellers, channeling their creativity into the overarching narrative.

Evolving Encores: The Dynamic Nature of Brand Evolution

The concluding chapter sets the stage for the future, detailing the significance of evolution in brand storytelling. Reflecting the ever-changing nature of society and consumer desires, learn how to revamp your brand narrative while staying true to your essence.

*Continuing the Symphony*: In an era marked by rapid changes, your brand's narrative must evolve to remain relevant.

Embrace transformation without losing sight of your core values, ensuring your brand symphony remains in tune with the shifting times.

Epilogue: Harmonizing Memories and Aspirations

This journey through brand storytelling and community building weaves an intricate tapestry, a harmonious blend of narratives and connections. As your brand's melody resonates through time, remember that its symphony will forever echo in the hearts and minds of those who resonate with its unique chords. The legacy is one of shared memories and soaring aspirations, a legacy that endures beyond the chapters themselves.

# CHAPTER 6: UNCONVENTIONAL STRATEGIES

*Dazzling Disruption: Pioneering Unorthodox Marketing*

Embark on a journey of marketing exploration that transcends convention. This chapter delves into the kaleidoscopic world of innovative marketing strategies that defy norms and captivate audiences in ways they never anticipated.

Enigmatic Experiences: Immersive Alternate Realities

Unleash the power of alternate realities to enrapture your audience. Discover how augmented reality (AR) and virtual reality (VR) weave a seamless blend of the tangible and the fantastical, creating immersive experiences that defy the boundaries of the ordinary.

*Reality Beyond Reality*: Augmented reality overlays digital elements onto the real world, while virtual reality offers complete immersion into an alternate universe. Both transform passive observers into active participants, forging connections through interactive engagement.

## Sensory Seduction: Multisensory Marketing

Elevate your marketing to the realm of sensory seduction. Engage your audience's senses beyond sight, leveraging touch, smell, taste, and sound to evoke emotional responses that etch your brand into their memories.

*Taste of Temptation*: By integrating taste and smell into your campaigns, you forge deep emotional connections that resonate. From scratch-and-sniff promotions to interactive culinary experiences, multisensory marketing intertwines your brand with unforgettable sensations.

## Empowering Micro-Moments: Marketing for Mobile Consumption

In a fast-paced digital landscape, micro-moments seize attention in a heartbeat. Master the art of crafting concise yet impactful content that captures the essence of your brand and resonates with the on-the-go audience.

*Moments of Magnitude*: Capitalize on fleeting moments where users turn to their devices for quick answers and insights.

From "how-to" videos to succinct social media stories, these micro-moments create a steady stream of engagement that aligns with modern attention spans.

## Gamification Galore: Transforming Engagement into Play

Infuse elements of play into your marketing strategy, unlocking a world of gamification that entices and entertains. Learn how turning mundane interactions into captivating games can forge deeper connections with your audience.

*The Playful Quest*: Transform user engagement into an exhilarating adventure. Rewarding challenges, interactive quizzes, and loyalty programs create a sense of achievement, nurturing a bond between your brand and the participants in your marketing game.

Whispers of Mystery: Cryptic Marketing Teasers

Mystique and curiosity intermingle in the realm of cryptic marketing. Unveil the secrets behind crafting enigmatic teasers and campaigns that compel your audience to engage, speculate, and unravel the narrative you've woven.

*Cryptic Enchantment*: Embrace the allure of the unknown, captivating your audience with breadcrumbs of intrigue. From encrypted messages to symbolic visuals, cryptic marketing kindles curiosity, beckoning participants to become part of your brand's unfolding mystery.

Empathy-Powered Marketing: Advocacy for Social Causes

Harness the potential of empathy-driven marketing, aligning your brand with meaningful social causes. By fostering a genuine connection between your brand's values and societal issues, you resonate with an audience that seeks to make a positive impact.

*The Compassionate Connection*: Embrace the role of an advocate, lending your voice to social issues that align with your brand's ethos. When your marketing campaigns champion change, you tap into the collective desire for a better world, aligning your brand with purposeful action.

Nostalgia Reimagined: Resurrecting the Past

Rekindle nostalgia through a modern lens, inviting your audience on a journey through time.

Learn how reviving elements of the past can evoke fond memories while infusing a sense of novelty into your brand.

*Past-Present Fusion*: Seamlessly blend nostalgia with innovation, invoking a sense of familiarity while presenting a fresh perspective. Retro-inspired designs, throwback references, and reinvented classics forge a bridge between generations and cultures.

Inclusive Innovation: Marketing for Diverse Audiences

Inclusivity transcends mere representation—it embraces authenticity and empathy. Embrace diversity in your marketing, ensuring your campaigns reflect the rich tapestry of humanity and resonate with a wide spectrum of audiences.

*Beyond Stereotypes*: Cultivate a genuine understanding of various cultures, orientations, and identities. From diverse casting to narratives that celebrate uniqueness, inclusive marketing bridges the gap between brand and consumer by honoring the individual.

The Trailblazing Crossover: Collaborative Marketing Fusion

Step into the world of collaborative marketing, where unexpected alliances birth innovation.

Discover how partnering with unlikely industries can create unique narratives that enchant and astonish your audience.

*The Fusion Phenomenon*: Unite your brand with others from distant realms, creating narratives that infuse each partner's essence into an enthralling tapestry. The result? An unexpected symphony that resonates across multiple spheres of interest.

## Epilogue: A Spectrum of Imagination

As the boundaries of conventional marketing blur into a spectrum of imagination, remember that the canvas of creativity knows no limits. Every strategy, whether rooted in reality or leaping beyond, has the power to captivate, inspire, and etch your brand's narrative into the hearts and minds of your audience. The ever-changing landscape awaits your ingenuity, inviting you to paint bold strokes of innovation and forge connections that transcend the ordinary.

# CHAPTER 7: BRAND STORIES

*Unveiling the Narrative Palette: The Power of Brand Storytelling*

Embark on a journey through the realm of brand storytelling—a canvas where words, visuals, and emotions intertwine to create narratives that resonate deep within the hearts of your audience.

Chronicles of Origin: Unraveling the Genesis Tale

Trace back the roots of your brand, unearthing the stories that birthed its existence. Delve into the lives and inspirations of its creators, revealing the authentic essence that breathes life into your brand's narrative.

*The Genesis Arc*: Every brand has a tale of inception, a narrative that echoes the passion, challenges, and aspirations that set its course. From a kitchen table idea to a garage-born invention, the origin story becomes the cornerstone of relatability, forging connections with those who seek the genuine and the human.

Mythos and Metaphor: Infusing Symbolism into Your Brand

Transcend the surface of your brand, delving into the realm of mythos and metaphor. Learn how weaving symbolism and allegory into your brand's narrative can elevate its meaning and resonate on a deeper level.

*Symbolic Rhapsody*: Align your brand with archetypes and metaphors that echo throughout cultures and history. From the phoenix's rebirth to the hero's journey, infusing these timeless narratives into your brand creates an intricate tapestry of meaning that resonates with the subconscious.

Characters of Resonance: Forging Personas and Ambassadors

Evoke empathy and connection by giving your brand a relatable face. Dive into the art of crafting personas and ambassadors that embody the spirit of your brand, becoming beacons of authenticity and resonance.

*Persona Portraits*: Whether it's the friendly neighbor next door or the daring adventurer seeking the unknown, personas humanize your brand, giving it relatable qualities that forge bonds.

Ambassadors, on the other hand, are real-life embodiments of your brand's values, amplifying its impact through their actions and advocacy.

Narrative Immersion: Creating Interactive Storyworlds

Unleash the magic of immersive storytelling, inviting your audience to step into a world of narrative wonder. Discover how interactive campaigns and experiential marketing create an environment where your audience becomes part of the story.

*Journey into the Story*: Transport your audience from passive observers to active participants through interactive narratives. From escape room experiences that unfold in real time to choose-your-own-adventure social media campaigns, the world of immersive storytelling transforms marketing into an engaging journey.

## Echoes of Emotion: Crafting Emotional Resonance

Explore the symphony of emotions that resonate within your audience, and master the art of weaving emotional threads into your brand narrative. Learn how the chords of joy, nostalgia, empathy, and even vulnerability can create harmonies that linger in memory.

*Emotional Tapestry*: Emotions are universal connectors, and your brand's narrative is the loom upon which they're woven. Whether it's evoking childhood nostalgia or addressing shared struggles, emotions bind your audience to your brand, leaving an indelible mark on their hearts.

## The Saga of Authenticity: Honesty in Brand Storytelling

Navigate the treacherous waters of authenticity, where truth and transparency reign supreme. Uncover how sharing the unvarnished truth—flaws and all—can resonate more powerfully than a carefully polished façade.

*Unveiled Humanity*: Audiences crave sincerity in a world saturated with glossy facades. By showcasing the unscripted, imperfect moments behind your brand's scenes, you connect on a level that says, "We're real, just like you."

## Storytelling Alchemy: Transforming Struggles into Triumphs

Breathe life into your brand narrative by embracing the alchemy of transformation.

Uncover how weaving tales of overcoming adversity and challenges can empower your audience and inspire them to triumph over their own hurdles.

*Resilience Reimagined*: Share stories of challenges faced and conquered, weaving a narrative of resilience and growth. From setbacks to triumphs, these tales become mirrors that reflect your audience's own struggles, lighting a path to their personal victories.

Unwritten Futures: Inviting Your Audience to Co-Create

Embark on a collaborative journey as you invite your audience to become co-authors of your brand's story. Discover the magic of co-creation, where shared experiences and collective narratives bind your brand with your audience's aspirations.

*Shared Horizons*: By letting your audience contribute to your brand narrative, you foster a sense of ownership and belonging. From user-generated content campaigns to interactive platforms that crowdsource ideas, co-creation transforms your audience into fellow storytellers.

Finale: The Symphony of Narratives

As we draw the curtains on this exploration of brand storytelling, remember that each narrative is a brushstroke in the masterpiece that is your brand's identity. By embracing the art of storytelling, you forge connections that transcend transactional exchanges, weaving a tapestry of emotions, dreams, and shared experiences that resonate for generations to come. The story of your brand is an unfolding symphony—one that captures hearts, ignites imaginations, and leaves an indelible mark on the world.

# CHAPTER 8: BRIDGING BRANDS AND COMMUNITIES

*Forging Strong Bonds: How Brands and Communities Come Together*

In today's interconnected world, brands are on a mission to build communities that go beyond just business transactions. They're creating spaces where people can connect over shared values.

Building a Community: Connecting People with a Common Purpose

Imagine brands as architects of communities, creating a place where people with similar values gather and form a bond that's more than just about buying things.

*Shared Identity*: Think of it like building a puzzle. Brands and community members have pieces that fit together perfectly, creating a bigger picture. Learn how to build a strong bond by sharing what you both stand for.

People Power: How Everyone Can Contribute

Ever heard of people who love a brand so much they become part of its story? That's what user-generated content is all about—when regular folks become storytellers for your brand.

*Sharing Stories*: Think of it as a giant scrapbook filled with memories. We'll show you how to get your community excited about sharing their own stories, turning them into brand ambassadors and adding a personal touch to your brand.

Heartfelt Conversations: Talking Like Friends, Not Marketers

Have you ever had a real, honest conversation with a brand? It's like chatting by a virtual campfire, sharing stories and advice.

*Authentic Talks*: Imagine a cozy chat with a close friend. Dive into the art of real conversations, where being genuine and really listening can create a bond that lasts.

People Who Matter: Influencers and Ambassadors

You know those people everyone looks up to? They can help your brand's message reach more people. It's like having popular friends who believe in what you do.

*Trusted Allies*: Think of them as your brand's cheerleaders. Discover how working with people who resonate with your community can help spread your message far and wide.

Working Together: Creating New Ideas as a Team

Ever thought about working with your customers to come up with cool new stuff? Co-creation is like a brainstorming session where everyone's ideas matter.

*Team Spirit*: Imagine a workshop where everyone throws in their suggestions. We'll show you how to get your community involved in creating new things that they'll love.

Growing and Learning: How Communities Shape Brands

Imagine if your customers could help you make your products better. It's like getting advice from your friends on what to cook for dinner.

*Feedback Loop*: Think of it as a suggestion box that's always open. Explore how involving your community in shaping your products can make them even more awesome.

Real Connections: Turning Online Friends into Real Ones

Ever wanted to meet the people you talk to online? Brands are hosting events where online connections turn into real friendships.

*Offline Adventures*: Think of it as a big party where everyone knows each other. We'll guide you on how to bring your digital community together in real life for unforgettable experiences.

Staying Strong: Keeping the Community Alive

As we wrap up our journey through community-building, remember that it's an ongoing adventure. By staying engaged, talking openly, and creating together, you're not just building a brand—you're creating a space where people feel like they belong.

In this digital world, the power of community is like a glue that holds everyone together, no matter where they are. So keep the conversations going, keep creating connections, and watch your brand and its community grow together.

Special Offer!

**Loved Our Book? We're Excited To Give Back To Our Loyal Fans!**

**Get 5 Exclusive Digital Books For Free.**

**Email: infobookpub@Gmail.Com With**

**The Subject As "Free Books"**

www.ingramcontent.com/pod-product-compliance
Lightning Source LLC
Chambersburg PA
CBHW072225290526
45794CB00007B/2893